Day Crafting
The Introductory
Workbook

**Foundations for the daily practice
of making a good life**

By **Bruce Stanley**

Day Crafting – The Introductory Workbook is the first book
from the Apprentice Series and is a pre-requisite for any further
workbook in the series.

Also in the Apprentice Series:

> **Day Crafting: The Body-clock Workbook**
> **Day Crafting: The Productivity Workbook**
> **Day Crafting: The Self-care Workbook**
> **Day Crafting: The Change Workbook**

Second edition, October 2023.

ISBN: 978-1-7398268-0-2

Published and designed by Embody Interactive – www.embody.co.uk
Day Crafting™ is a registered trademark.

Contents

Day Crafting

Day Crafting is about developing the skills to use time meaningfully; it is the everyday art of making a good life. It is a set of methods to craft the *style* in lifestyle.

How is your day different from how it could have been? Bridging that gap is the skill of Day Crafting.

It is the good life in two steps: balance and flourish today, then repeat tomorrow.

You will need

- Time and space to learn and some problems to solve.
- A (developing) craftsperson's mindset.
- A handy notebook. I use a hard-backed dotted notebook with a ribbon – with pages roughly the size and design of the page opposite. There are some blank pages at the end of this workbook if you don't have a separate notebook handy.

It's a *Work*book

It isn't a book intended to be read in a hurry. You will get the most out of this by taking your time and applying the practises to your own life – and by putting the work in. An example pace might be roughly two weeks practicing with the basic tools before you get to halfway through the workbook at page 55.

Bruce Stanley

A little about me ... I'm a designer, innovation facilitator, product manager and adult education specialist. I've been developing personal growth and positive psychology products for many years – I consider myself *a purveyor of fine aha moments*.

Thank you so much for joining me in the Day Crafting workshop; let's go and make something and have fun in the process.

To you from Day Crafting apprentices

" I thoroughly enjoy Day Crafting. As a mum of three and running two businesses, I often found my days just filled up and I ended up feeling overwhelmed and having little time for what I would like to be doing. I made a very radical step of scheduling a 2-hour lunch break, including a nap and a walk, making me far more productive. I wouldn't have even considered this an option before.
Rosie Freeman. Therapist

Day Crafting has helped me create life-giving daily rhythms and confidence in how to schedule my days best. The simple tool of setting an intention can lead to a day that feels more giving and constructive. There is so much more to learn through Day Crafting, which makes for exciting days.
Matt Freer. Project Manager

I decided to start Day Crafting because, having retired, I had some time on my hands for the first time. It was not that I could not find things to fill the time – I am never bored – but I wanted to be more intentional about how I used my time. I wanted to craft the life I wanted rather than drift into a different sort of busyness. Day Crafting is excellent! What sets this apart from other methods is partly the concept and the superb course material. The material is well thought through, interesting and beautifully produced. A few months since starting, Day Crafting has helped me live more intentionally.
Maya Bimson. Retired

Future you doesn't really exist. What are you postponing that you can **experience** today?

Goals don't produce results, only practise does. What practise can you devote **today** to?

Time, not money is critical to your **happiness**. How can you wisely invest your time today?

The happiest we can be is today. What's the simplest thing you can do **now** to raise your wellbeing?

The good life is not arrived at, it is only experienced now. How can you **craft** a good day?

Life improves when you can craft each day you're living. What skills and tools do you need to craft today?

Why learn Day Crafting?

Crafting higher quality time
Day Crafting develops the skilled use of time, which is a much better enabler of happiness and flourishing than money or possessions. Imagine days when more gets done without feeling overly busy, and there is room for the slow appreciation of good things such as food, music, and connection with friends and family.

Remodelling health and balance
Day Crafting deliberately balances all of us: the different aspects of our day, energy rhythms, and interior and exterior life. Rest is as important as working. Deep work is as important as deep play.

Growing through process
Developing and strengthening positive identity through craftwork methodologies is a different model for change, emphasising the accumulation of small wins and meaningful progress measured daily rather than focusing on future and momentary milestones.

Forming skills and confidence
Living your days well and skilfully rewards you with a sense of pride and strengthens a positive identity and personality. Every day that you make meaningful progress feels energising, empowering and freeing.

Forging memorable moments

Particular moments from special days are the highlights of the story of our lives – novel experiences or moments of awe or pride. Days to remember forever. These days don't need to be left to chance; they can be deliberately crafted, and every Day Crafting apprentice should be able to design these blueprints.

Reshaping career and productivity

Being time and energy centric through Day Crafting can make you, ironically, *more* productive and successful in your career than being money and status-orientated. With this shift comes pro-social benefits and better relationships with colleagues and customers.

Day Crafting is a craft, so welcome to the workshop

Craft vocabulary is in everyday speech, such as form follows function, fitness for purpose, broad brushes, frames of reference, shaping, palettes, the working surface and the cutting edge.

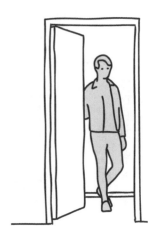

Day Crafting uses the language, concepts, rhythms, values and philosophy of craftwork as a frame. As a potter, carpenter or mason is to their material, so a Day Crafter is to their day.

Traditional ethos, modern application. Craft practice now embraces new disciplines, including coding, photography and writing, to name a few, and the badge 'craft' stamps various products with a distinct value, e.g. craft cheese or craft beer.

And craft is not synonymous with shaping physical materials. As far back as the 6th century, some monastics described their communities as 'workshops' and their rules as 'tools'.

Craftwork has always included *soul-craft* as a side effect; the maker is shaped by shaping. None of that is lost in Day Crafting.

Practical exercises from this workbook

Let's get started. Day Crafting is one-part theory to five-parts practical. Just like any craft skill, you learn by doing.

Throughout this workbook you will see these **four icons.** They represent opportunities and suggestions for action intended to help you learn, design and reflect, and develop skill.

This icon represents an **exercise to complete in your own notebook.** In Day Crafting, your notebook is called **Design Notes.**

This indicates an **exercise to complete directly in *this* workbook.** Space is provided (you can use your Design Notes instead).

This indicates a **practical activity** to design into your day. The bulk of Day Crafting is in the doing.

And this is an **idea or question** to give some thought to. Hold it in your mind to shape and develop.

How is your day going?

We're asked this question occasionally by other people – and by ourselves. Ask yourself this question now. If the day could be going better – how might you improve what remains of the day?

To explore the question further, imagine viewing a dashboard representing you and your day. What would it show right now – how would the gauges read?

Draw a pointer on each of these scales representing you now

Low or no **energy**, exhausted	High **energy**, flourishing
Distracted, **unproductive**	As **productive** as I want to be
The day is out of **balance**	Contented, the day is **balanced**
Uncontrolled **mental state**	Controlled **mental state**
I have ignored my **self-care**	I have maximised **self-care**

What is **one small thing** you can do with what remains of today to improve one (or more) of these measurements? Write an idea in the space below.

print out lists

Even with simple **Day Crafting** skills, you should be able to steer your days towards the positive end of these scales. More good days add up to a good life and develop skills which strengthen the daily practice in a positive feedback loop.

What could you achieve with greater skill? Day Crafting is about developing the skills and enjoying the practice.

Learning, satisfaction and empowerment in the workshop

Your strongest motivations to learn come from within; they're *intrinsic* motivations. You're not learning because you have to but because you choose to. Entering the Day Crafting workshop can be creative, empowering, a flow state, playful and delightful.

What prompts us to learn, develop, improve or change? It could be a desire to *move towards* something better or *away from* something worse. Either way, the challenge comes into focus as **a creative problem to solve.**

 What problem are you **ready** to solve next?

You will be ready to engage in Day Crafting to the extent that you feel the need to learn and have identified a problem the learning will help you solve. Or you may sense that clarity will come from play and experimentation. You will invest energy in making use of these resources to the extent that you see them as being relevant to your needs.

Creative problems motivate learning

The learning in Day Crafting is not abstract theory or **instruction,** which may be the only learning model you've encountered before, typically in school. Adults learn best through a different model, by **constructing** their learning. The critical difference with *constructed learning* is that you are responsible for deciding what problems you want to solve and in what order; you'll decide what you're *ready* to learn next. You *construct* your learning.

The models are contrasted below.

There will be discrete opportunities for instruction, much as there would be on any craftwork course as we explore how to use new tools, but the *instruction* is within a *constructed* learning journey.

Construction	Instruction
Readiness to learn is problem oriented	Learning is subject oriented
Learning is sequenced and paced by the student	Content and pace is decided by the teacher
Learning needs are diagnosed by the learner	Learning needs are diagnosed by teacher
Learning is put into practise immediately	Postponed application of learning
Integrates previous experience	Learner starting from scratch
Experimentation and play are encouraged	Assigned learning tasks
Facilitated by catalyst or guide	Led by teacher or instructor

Being an adult doesn't automatically orientate you to construct your learning; it takes responsibility. We may be out of practice or have never found our identity as adult learners. We may expect to be told what to do, but for an adult Apprentice, that rarely leads to a fulfilling experience, and no practice gets done; if learning feels like *I-have-to-do*, it quickly becomes *I-didn't-do*.

Keep it simple

You shouldn't get lost or overwhelmed by Day Crafting; if you're unsure what to do next, the solution-focused question is: **'What simple thing can I do now or today?'.**

My life is dull and boring

I'm close to burnout, I have low energy all the time

Possible starting points

My to-do list is overwhelming

I set and achieve goals but never seem to find happiness

My rest doesn't seem to replenish me

I'm no longer being productive

I have no spare time

I don't feel like I'm ever really present

for the
Apprentice
Day Crafter

I can't break bad habits

I don't give myself permission to prioritize self-care

My life feels out of balance

I never seem to get to the things I love doing

Problem hunting

Try this exercise: think through an average of recent days and rate each broad area by ticking one of the boxes on each row. E.g. if you haven't slept well in the last week, you might tick the middle column. Some headings are open to interpretation; what they mean is up to you.

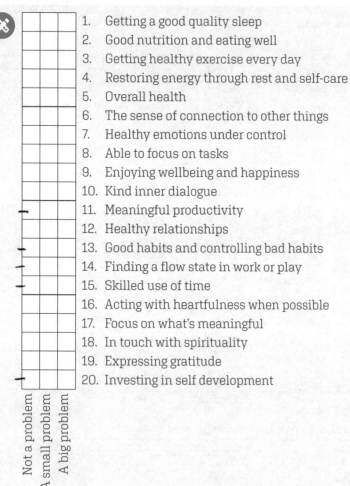

1. Getting a good quality sleep
2. Good nutrition and eating well
3. Getting healthy exercise every day
4. Restoring energy through rest and self-care
5. Overall health
6. The sense of connection to other things
7. Healthy emotions under control
8. Able to focus on tasks
9. Enjoying wellbeing and happiness
10. Kind inner dialogue
11. Meaningful productivity
12. Healthy relationships
13. Good habits and controlling bad habits
14. Finding a flow state in work or play
15. Skilled use of time
16. Acting with heartfulness when possible
17. Focus on what's meaningful
18. In touch with spirituality
19. Expressing gratitude
20. Investing in self development

Not a problem
A small problem
A big problem

Here are a few provocative backup questions for problem-hunting if the exercise above doesn't work for you. Ask yourself: what is broken in your days that you'd like to fix, or is there a mistake you make regularly that you'd like to remedy, or what's the first thing you'd change to improve your days?

Problem selection

It may be that several issues from the list are **big** problems, and you might feel ready to work on one or two – or your self-development instincts might be attracted to improving an area where you're already strong; this is fine too – the issue you work on is up to you*.

You can shape your understanding and motivation around a few candidate problems by thinking through or writing about (in your Design Notes) the following questions concerning the issue.

1. **How important is this issue?**
2. **What would solving this problem do for you?**
3. **What would others notice about you if you solved this?**
4. **Is this within your power to change?**
5. **What might the barriers be?**

* an obvious drawback to consider when selecting problems is your bias towards selecting ones that attract you. On the one hand, you need to work on what you're ready and motivated to engage with, but are you also making wise, kind and balanced choices? Maybe you're drawn to challenging and self-critical problems because you're too tough on yourself and like giving yourself a hard time. Perhaps the opposite is the case, and you select only easy or urgent problems and ignore the complex or important ones. How can you address these risks? Sometimes, working with guidance or with fellow apprentices can help widen your perspective.

Also, some big and significant problems shouldn't be up for debate – you *should* look for a solution (and even seek professional help or advice where relevant) with any of the following: chronic sleep issues, health issues, chronic stress, self-sabotaging habits, poor diet, not enough exercise, addiction, mental health issues and legal or financial problems.

From problem to *how might I ...?*

You may need to reshape your problems to allow your creative design thinking to work on experiments and solutions.

How do you hear yourself describe problems – does your default language have you believing you're trapped with no hope of a solution, or are you instantly firing up your creativity?

Two things happen at this stage; firstly, problems are chunked down into units small enough to make simple experiments out of. More importantly, they're reframed as **how might I** ... questions, or **HMI** ... for short (or how might we, if in a group). A single problem, such as 'I'm too busy', should become multiple HMI questions.

Some real-world problems suggested by Day Crafting apprentices have been reframed as these example HMI questions.

> HMI work out what problem I'm ready for next?
> HMI work out what my main constraints
> for change and improvement are?
> HMI work out the simplest changes I can make
> for the biggest improvements to my days?
> HMI easily tell if I am making improvements?
> HMI find the best time of day for (various activities)?
> HMI bring my focus from future worries to the present?
> HMI find out what I love doing?
> HMI increase my motivation?
> HMI help myself sleep better at night?
> HMI make more time for myself?
> HMI figure out what I should do with my life?
> HMI structure my day for (various outcomes)?
> HMI prioritise my time to achieve more?

Instead of feeling beaten, each of these reframes can have you fizzing with creative ideas. Each HMI can become a list of possible experiments to run to see if they solve the problem. **One problem becomes multiple HMI questions. Each HMI question can become multiple experiments** and you choose the experiment you're motivated by and able to test.

This process around *problems that you're ready to solve* will become internalised and automatic. The exercises here are designed to highlight and understand the constructed learning model, they are not meant to be practised repeatedly after you've absorbed the learning – unless you want to.

Take one of your problems through this process. Use the space on this page to practise your design thinking and try the process out. You could use a problem you've highlighted from the *Problem Hunting* exercise on page 16.

1) Write a single problem here

2) Reframe the problem into multiple HMI questions

3) Generate some small and specific experiment ideas from one or two of the HMI questions

E.g. Problem: **I'm too busy**, might become, HMI get less to do, HMI organise my to-do list, HMI get more done, HMI find more time ... and so on.

The first **HMI get less to do** might generate more HMIs or small specific experiments, behaviours or actions such as: HMI delegate some of my tasks? HMI choose what to delegate? Or, Talk to my manager tomorrow about my capacity. Practise saying 'no' to non-urgent or non-important tasks. Clarify my job description. ETC

We've got to an **experiment** – this is a good place to start Day Crafting ...

... but before carrying on, we're going to explore the **material** we're working with.

Material

**As Day Crafters, our material is
ourselves: our daily rhythms,
energy flows, habits, decisions,
motivations, thoughts,
behaviours and reactions.
Our circumstances, our
responsibilities and
our relationships. Our
interactions with others,
our environment and an
understanding of what is in
or out of our control.**

We don't need an advanced
understanding of the material to
begin Day Crafting – but we do
need a little knowledge and,
better still, wisdom to know
where to start working with the
material. What can we change,
and how? What properties are
mouldable, and how much
energy is required?

 Day Crafting teaches the skilled use of time and energy.

Craftspeople must know their material to understand best what it
can do, whether the material is wood, stone, metal, or even sugar,
ice, photos, words or code.

All of that material understanding is captured in the quality
of their work. Watching an experienced craftsperson work is
fascinating – we're perceiving a much deeper engagement than
merely the physical processes. *Craftwork is soul-craft.*

Over the following few pages, we will explore some interesting properties of the material. This content is a necessary foundation, and it will be worth referring back to it occasionally as you continue with the practical details of Day Crafting.

As you become more involved, these properties of the material may help you understand issues you run into if the *material* doesn't react in the way you expected.

Our energy budget

Think of your most passive, restful state, apart from sleeping, perhaps when you collapse on the sofa or sit waiting. Even when we're doing nothing, we are never doing nothing. When resting, the mind can be as busy as when fully active. What is the mind doing that you're not consciously thinking about and what does that have to do with energy availability?

Some extraordinary automatic functions are going on in our brains and bodies, which are monitored continually by our minds.

Our minds constantly look after us, keeping us alive and making predictions about what may lie ahead in our day, balanced with how much energy we have to respond if those *predictions* are correct. (Sometimes those predictions are habitually wrong, but that's a separate issue).

Your energy budget, predicting and managing energy reserves, subtly encourages you to follow routines and habits which are good at conserving energy.

Humans daily

20,000 breaths
100,000 heart beats
14,000 blinks
1/4 million eye movements
2,000+ calories processed
200 billion red blood cells created
180 ltr filtered by kidneys

Temperature calibrated
Immune system optimised
Hormones balanced
Status protected
Territory guarded
Dangers appraised
Potential mates identified
Parental care exercised
Hunger monitored
Tiredness signalled

This energy budgeting function has been with us throughout our evolution and has kept us alive long enough to reproduce and raise offspring within a food-gathering tribe.

In a process called **interoception,** at every moment of every day, this energy budget is being measured, monitored and managed. When all is fine, your conscious mind doesn't notice anything is going on. Still, we often notice when the budget is out of balance during the day: we catch a physiological message such as hunger or the appearance of a **mood** such as anxiety.

Whether a negative state exists or all is fine, you can 'read' your energy budget at any moment on a kind of dashboard. If you're quiet for a moment and tune into your current state, you can begin to check in on your state of **affect** quickly. *What you're reading is best described as a feeling or a mood; it isn't an emotion yet.*

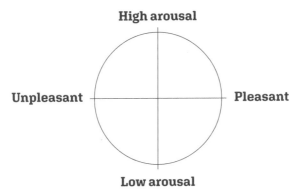

This is a helpful model (called the *Affective Circumplex*) for the Day Crafter who wants to develop greater self-awareness.

If you were to place a dot on your version of this dashboard right now, where would it be? Sketch it in your Design Notes.

A typical mood description for a bottom-right point, pleasant but low arousal, could be *calm*. The top right could be *excited*. The bottom left could be depressed, bored or tired. We have many words for the top left, such as restlessness, agitation, confusion, and fear. The centre is neutral, but how often are you here?

Where are you on this diagram by default? Does it depend on your circumstances?

This subject isn't a diversion; it is a practical, foundational theory for Day Crafting – **our desire for change, improvement and experimentation has to work within our available energy budget** – which might mean making more energy available or being more realistic about what we can achieve.

How much of your day is on autopilot?

Think of a habit as something you do with minimal conscious effort, something or a sequence of things you do on autopilot. When you consider the following routines in your own life, to what degree are they habitual?

 Write a percentage in each box. The more you assess you are on autopilot in this part of your day, the higher the %

Getting up and ready	%
Morning till lunchtime	%
Afternoons	%
Transition from work to leisure	%
Evenings	%
Interactions with friends / family	%
Interactions with colleagues	%
Inner dialogue, self-talk	%

There is no correct answer here; it is a self-assessment, but getting a second opinion from someone who knows you well may be interesting to see if their assessment of your habitualness is the same.

Some research suggests that 50% of our days are automatic, but most Day Crafting apprentices I have asked think this is low and would give themselves a higher percentage.

Other research shows that we're likely to be more habitual the older we get, but for most of us, there is also the desire for novelty, change and first-time experiences. This is one of the aspects we like about holidays in new places – but novelty and diversion from routine come at a cost to our energy budgets.

 Are you motivated to craft any of the above parts of your day?

Why are we habitual?

Managing our energy budget, which is primarily an automatic process, is central to our days whether we're aware of it or not. The goal of our energy budget is to make sure we have enough energy available, in the same way we would have needed energy if we were mesolithic food-gatherers: survival, nutrition, status in the tribe, territory, reaction to danger etc. This system is trying to keep us alive and it is working continually.

The system runs most efficiently when it's automatic, when we don't have to think, which is one of the roles of habits – things done automatically with very little conscious thought.

Most habits are essential and valuable and we're happy to keep those. Some are detrimental and harm us, and there are good habits we'd like to have but don't – both of these situations require us to change, to stop a harmful habit or to start a beneficial one – but change is tricky. It can affect the energy budget, which is fine if it's managed wisely. The subject of habit change is also a good source of problems for the Day Crafter.

What habit(s) would you like to stop? Name at least one.

What habit(s) would you like to start? Name at least one.

Elephant and Rider

A good simile is a helpful way to think about the automatic and controlled systems operating in our minds. This is my favourite.

If we imagine two systems – the conscious, controlled thinking system and the automatic habitual system – we can instinctively understand a lot about how they interact if we imagine them like a *rider* sitting on an *elephant*.

The elephant

This is our powerful, ancient, automatic (mostly) present self. It is very fast acting and can monitor multiple tasks simultaneously and by comparison to the rider, does so with little effort. It is where our energy budget is monitored. It is where our defence mechanisms are and it tends to *respond* rather than *think*. Sometimes, it can take over our thinking, and it tends to be opinionated, black and white, paranoid, catastrophic, irrational and give emotive judgements. For much of the time, it can be passive and calm, but it is capable of hijacking us – and as the simile makes obvious, it is much stronger than the rider. Your elephant doesn't care if you're happy; it is just trying to keep you alive.

The rider

This is a newer part of our brain. It evolved to serve the elephant, but in many situations, the rider thinks it is in control and can even deny all knowledge of the elephant and has to provide rational reasons for why we've behaved as if we were under the influence of ... an animal. The rider is our controlled, conscious, *one-think-at-a-time* system. It is our language, logical thinking, morals, empathy, and future planning. It is where we attempt to control the impulses of the elephant, where we try to change our habits. The rider cares if we're happy and makes inexpert guesses about how to achieve that, often disregarding the elephant's leanings.

Put into the context of Day Crafting, this is a critical part of understanding the **material** and our capacity for **changing it.**

The rider can be very aspirational, but if your rider designs a grand blueprint but doesn't allow for and work with the elephant, the elephant is likely to win any battle of wills, discipline or self-control. The rider plans future days, but the elephant, operating mainly in the present, wasn't part of the planning and makes it clear that it thinks the activity is a bad idea. But your rider can work around your elephant if you have the wisdom – if the rider doesn't buy the biscuits, the elephant can't eat the whole packet in one go – or is that just me?

Day Crafting is an elephant and rider friendly methodology. Small experiments tried today don't threaten the elephant.

Day Crafter's mindset

Behaviour change, even trying something tiny for one day that takes two minutes, can throw some of us off. You plan to do something, but when it comes to it, you don't. Putting this into elephant and rider terminology, the future, values-orientated rider thinks it'll be good to try something new. The here-and-now behavioural elephant can overrule the plan if the two are not aligned.

I will introduce another analogy helpful to Day Crafting by describing two contrasting **mindsets.** This is a separate but complementary concept to the elephant and rider. Give both ideas some thought and see which you find helpful.

The Labourer
'Today is happening *to me.*'

- Life is happening **to him**. The causes of whatever condition he is in are *outside* of him.

- He blames things external to him. You made me unhappy. The weather made me late. If my team worked harder, our company would do better.

- I didn't / couldn't do it because life got in the way.

- Often, something happening in the past is to blame.

- He says, why did this happen to me?

- The world *should* be a certain way ... and it's not ... and *something else* needs to change, not me.

- He makes his wellbeing dependent on external factors.

How do you get into this mindset?
How do you get out of this mindset?

These two mindsets, below, are states of consciousness illustrated by two craft-related identities, the Labourer and the Architect. You may prefer the contrast of actor and playwright or one of your invention.

They are not hierarchies or stages – we move from one to the other and regularly flip back again, sometimes in a matter of minutes.

Day Crafting is more about being in the **by-me** mindset whilst managing the fact that the **to-me** mindset is strong in us as well.

Putting it together: your mind has an elephant and rider mode, which may be aligned or not. If not, the elephant will probably get its way. Also, your view of your control over your days and your capacity to change may be like the Labourer or the Architect.

The Architect
'Today is happening *by me.*'

- From victim identity to creator identity.
- She is the primary cause of her experience.
- She can change her experience, interpretation of events, time use, happiness, productivity ...
- She says the way things are is excellent for my learning.
- Life gets in the way, but she expects that and plans around it, defending what she identified previously as valuable.
- She chooses to accept and take responsibility for whatever is occurring.
- However, only sometimes is the world the way she wants it to be.

What enables you to stay in this mindset? How do you switch from the Labourer to the Architect?

Process over product

Many methodologies help with personal development or accomplishment or making change and improvement by moving towards something better. Or they work remedially by moving away from something worse. Day Crafting fits into this space, but to be clear, it does not focus on defining a future state or **the product.**

Nearly everyone can imagine exciting future goals – the rider is good at this – but it is another skill altogether to affect the quality of the day we are actually in, ***the process.*** This is the behavioural cutting edge, the working surface where we actually are.

The Day Crafter makes a good life from good todays – this is where the practice is – and where the challenge is.

Culture tells the wrong story about success and flourishing. Results have very little to do with the future goals we set and nearly everything to do with the systems of practice we have in place – the craftwork – which is why Day Crafting places today above tomorrow. It is a liberating shift: when the process is more important than the result, you play. When the result is more important than the process, you work.

Future aims and outcomes exist for the Day Crafter – imagine a sketch of a finished piece – but only in as much as they help clarify direction when clarity is needed.

The future goal is de-emphasised.

After all, it is achieved in one moment on one day, and often, it doesn't provide the present us (mostly elephant) with what future imagining us (mostly rider) thought it would when we planned it.

A Day Crafted life aims to make every day count.

The coaching model of goals and winning and being the best means that the further we progress, the fewer of us there are – but craftwork doesn't fit this framework; it is egalitarian. We can all be craftspeople and develop skill and mastery without competition or comparison – and in service to those around us.

Instead of thinking, what is the meaning of my life?
Think, how can I make today meaningful?

Instead of thinking, what future state will make me happy?
Think, how can I craft time for this today?

Instead of thinking, what should I add to my bucket list?
Think, how can I fully experience today?

Instead of thinking, how can I make more money?
Think, how can I release more time?

Instead of thinking, who do I want to become?
Think, how can I be like this today?

Instead of thinking, how am I ever going to finish this?
Think, how can I break the task into day size chunks?

Instead of thinking, how can I cope with the fear of big changes?
Think, what small change can I experiment with today?

Instead of thinking, what is urgent?
Think, what is important?

Instead of thinking, what should I know about the future?
Think, what problem can I solve today?

Instead of thinking, how can I win the game?
Think, how can I practise better?

Instead of thinking, how can I keep everyone else happy?
Think, how can I make time for what I need today?

Instead of thinking, how can I face tomorrow?
Think, how can I make rest and self-care effective today?

Instead of thinking, what great results should I focus on?
Think, how can I channel my energy into better practice?

Instead of thinking, how do I make a successful innovation?
Think, how do I do brilliant innovating?

Instead of thinking, when will I arrive?
Think, how do I take the next step?

A recap of the main points

We've taken a brief but important diversion from the practical problem-based steps in section one (you ended up with experiment ideas). The Day Crafting work will continue in the next section, but the additional theories should inform your thinking.

- **Constructed learning.** The first section's main point was to clarify how adults learn best: through identifying problems you're motivated to take on.
- **Energy budget limits what you can do.** Each of us is limited in our capacity to change and divert from our default behaviours by our energy budget.
- **Working with both elephant and rider.** In certain circumstances our thinking can be conflicted between two modes, one deep and automatic – one controlled and logical.
- **Labourer or Architect mindset.** The day is happening 'to me', or the day is happening 'by me'. We can shift our mindset into a more productive identity.
- **Focus on Process.** Day Crafting work emphasises the value of the system of practice, the process, rather than the future goal.

How does this apply to you?

The following exercise is concise but does help you to think about the relevance of each of these subjects to you.

The first of each question pairs opposite asks you to think about how you observe this subject in your own life; where is the evidence? And the second asks you to reflect on what you learn from that. It may highlight where you need further reflection or knowledge.

If you would like to explore any of these with more space than is provided here, your Design Notes is a good option.

Constructed Learning page 12

How I observe this:

From that I learn:

Energy Budget page 24

How I observe this:

From that I learn:

Elephant & Rider page 28

How I observe this:

From that I learn:

Labourer / Architect Mindset page 30

How I observe this:

From that I learn:

Focus on Process page 32

How I observe this:

From that I learn:

Next we get really
practical and
introduce some
tools.

Use the tools.
Get involved.
Learn by doing.

Become the **maker**
of your days.

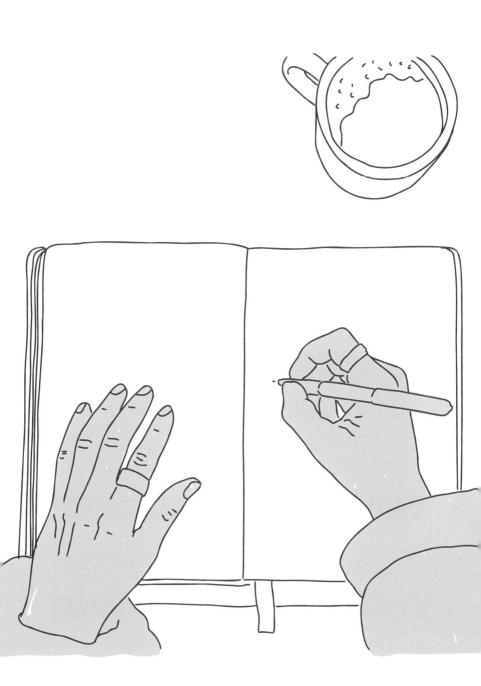

Apprentice Tools

Day Crafting practice uses a load of hacks, interventions, habits and exercises – otherwise known as **tools.** Each tool has a precise use or set of uses – much like any tool in a craftsperson's workshop. They can have unexpected benefits; using tools will teach you. You'll use some tools repeatedly and others only occasionally, if ever. And you can adapt tools; I've never been in a craftsperson's workshop and have not seen homemade tools.

Tools become the next step in the problem-experiment-learn process. Previously, you took problems through a process, developing HMI lists and then experimenting with ideas – this process can become the source for what you use Day Crafting tools to work on. The problem / experiment informs your tool choice.

Try tools out. This is important. Be open-minded and get practical with a beginner's mind. Sometimes a new, simple tool can dramatically change the quality of your days and your life.

Here is your first tool – which is a notebook:

Tool: Design Notes

When I begin and end most days, I want to quickly see what's important and where *Meaningful Progress* is happening, so that I can stay motivated and more wisely find insights and see what I might be overlooking. It is useful for externalising thoughts.

I also love the action of making notes on paper which links me to all craftspeople; we all share this practice.

What is it:

A Day Crafting *journal*. I use a hardback dotted notebook with a ribbon. Dots are more versatile than lines and can be used for diagrams and tables. My notebook is about the size of a novel, 11.5 x 18 cm. (Use whatever you prefer).

Use it to:

Use it for *design* and *review*; for design thinking and measurements, ideas and reflections. Making notes transfers your thoughts from your mind to the page which frees up cognitive resources. Many other Day Crafting tools will use **Design Notes.**

Design – Craft – Review

The crafted day has two distinct elements, **design** thinking (which includes **review** activities) and the **craftwork** itself.

Craftwork accounts for the bulk of the day with design being an optional or periodic activity used to solve a problem, set direction or discover insight.

> **Design** is thinking, sketching and planning. It is about becoming intentional and creative about the day ahead.
>
> **Craft** is the practical activities and behaviours undertaken to realise a design; *doing* the day itself.
>
> **Review** completes the loop. This is time to assess the quality of the craft done and the skill used in the work.

Design typically happens ahead of the craftwork, and design-*review* happens afterwards. **A day might follow this pattern across the waking hours:**

The time taken for both design activities, at the start and end of the day, could take only a few minutes – but depending on the craftwork underway and the problems to be solved, more time designing and reviewing returns more learning, insight and clarity.

As an option some people prefer to put both design aspects of Day Crafting in the evening. In this example, the current day's craft-work is reviewed and then the following day is planned.

But design as an activity isn't compulsory every day. If a crafts-person has work that spans a number of days, design thinking can happen as necessary. I always have my **Design Notes** handy for this scenario; my focus is craftwork, but I may often jot ideas down or clarify process when needed.

Review yesterday ...

Write, draw, doodle, diagram, flow-chart, cartoon ...

Design
tomorrow ...

Sketch, graph, word-associate, mind-map, list, measure ...

No-one said your design notes needed to just be lines of text!

Intention setting

Intention setting is the most frequently used Day Crafting tool for many apprentices. It solves a problem we have in most of our days, which is clarifying what the highlight should be.

This is not necessarily about getting more done; it is about deciding the focus or most satisfying part of the day ahead of time. Once that is determined, your elephant and rider can be aligned, and you'll have more energy in your thinking.

Improving your days is a case of being intentional with your free and work time. An intention might be about achieving satisfaction or delight as much as getting the urgent or important done.

At the heart of intention setting is the satisfaction of exercising control and autonomy, exercising our intrinsic motivations. It is also the simplest way to progress on anything momentous – the product is nothing without the actual craftwork.

Intention setting is an antidote to malaise. It is easy to end days feeling like time, or opportunity was wasted, that we were unfocussed, or that we were on autopilot – what is in common with those days is that we *weren't* intentional. Setting intentions is a simple and quick tool to use with long-reaching beneficial effects, and each day is a refresh; you're not setting an intention for the rest of your life; it is just for one day.

Of course, setting the intention is just the start; we've still got to do whatever the intended behaviour was or learn from why we didn't.

Suggested Practise

The objective is for you to learn how useful this tool is – how it affects your days and how it fits with your elephant and rider dynamic.

I recommend setting an intention every morning for at least a week or two, and I encourage you to find other opportunities in your days to set intentions.

Tool: Day's Intention

At the start of the day (or activity), I want to focus on what's important so that I can end the day satisfied that I've made Meaningful Progress. I am also often surprised and delighted by intentions that jump out at me.

What is it:

A numbered list of precise or open intentions that give the day ahead, or the activity ahead one simple focus. I use mine most days in my Design Notes; they are copied onto the first page.

1. **What is most important to get done today?**
2. **For today to be great I need to ...?**
3. **What passion have I neglected that I can do today?**
4. **What can I do more of that makes me happy today?**
5. **How do I want to feel at the end of today?**
6. **What do I need to reserve energy for today?**
7. **How might I protect my emotions today?**
8. **What am I putting off that I should get on with?**
9. **What good can I do today?**
10. **Who could use my support today and how?**

Use it to:

Choose one **Intention** to make progress or quickly focus yourself ahead of a day or activity. Also use it as a creative prompt for actions and behaviours you may otherwise forget about. Write the number you have chosen and a brief description in your **Design Notes** (page 38) for the day, example below.

Tuesday 2 Nov 2021

2 Read some of my new book

Honing Intention practice

Do you sometimes forget to carry out the intentions you set? Everything is clear when you're in the design phase of the day, when you're setting the intention, but the elephant ... or distractions, or life gets in the way and you end up not getting what you intended done. There are two optional details that you can add to the intentions you design to help increase success.

1. Getting specific with Intentions

This first option isn't complicated. It requires you to come up with some precise additional information about your Day's Intention. This can turn a *weak* intention into a *strong* one and dramatically increase your likelihood of carrying it out. The technique asks you to specify your intention's *what, when* and *where*. It works by stretching your design thinking to include more specific details around your intention, which then may happen more automatically.

I will **do intention** at **time** in **location.**

The intention from the previous page could now look like this:

Tuesday 2 Nov 2021

2 | I will read some of my new book at 7.30pm in the kitchen

It is also worth considering your overall motivation. Your intention is made by your future-planning rider, who has one set of motivations; it may be refused by your elephant, who has another set. E.g. It comes to the time when you intended to do something, but now you *don't feel like it.* One solution to this is to be clear at the time of intention setting what the *overall* effective motivations for it are to satisfy the rider *and* elephant.

Thinking through intention fails

What kinds of intentions do you often forget to do or easily sideline when other things get in the way? What do you intend to do that you rarely manage to do? For example, I intend to practice playing an instrument but I often allow other things to get in the way.

2. Linking intentions to existing habits

This second strategy is as simple as the first but works slightly differently. It works *because* we're habitual and on autopilot for much of our days, as we explored on page 26.

A possible problem with remembering to do an intention is that it is novel and doesn't already have a position in our automatic sequence of behaviours. As such, it is easily forgotten or bypassed. When you think about the automatic sequences of habits you follow in your days, you don't have to remember to eat breakfast, put your socks on or lock the door when you leave because they're all parts of well-rehearsed sequences. The morning routine is triggered by the alarm going off and a series of discrete behaviours are activated as the previous one ends.

Behaviour chaining, as it's called, uses this process to lodge a *new* intention *just after* one you know you're going to do already – because you always do.

After I do **regular behaviour,** I will **do intention.**

The example intention could now look like this:

> Tuesday 2 Nov 2021
>
> 2 After I load the dishwasher, I will read some of my new book

Try to be precise about the ending of the previous routine. I described the end of my routine as 'after I *load* the dishwasher' because, in my case, that is the end; I don't put the dishwasher on until the morning. But in someone else's case, it could be, 'after I turn the dishwasher on'. Or with another example, it wouldn't be 'after I get home'; it would be 'after I've taken my outside shoes off ...' Try to think precisely about the last behaviour of the preceding activity to trigger the new intention.

Don't forget you can apply this to the Day's Intention tool itself. *After I do ... I will set the Intention for the day.*

List 10+ of your possible cues

Go through your day and detail the end point of your regular behaviours, which may be perfect slots for new intentions, E.g., After
putting my toothbrush back on the holder. Or After I put the car
key in the ignition. Or when I finish my second coffee.

Meaningful Progress

This tool is the perfect partner to Day's Intention; achieving your intention might be that day's Meaningful Progress.

In a study, Teresa Amabile, Director of Research at Harvard Business School, examined the daily diaries of hundreds of people to determine what motivational forces were in play when they were delivering their best creative and productive performance. She found that of the five most commonly identified motivational factors (recognition, incentives, interpersonal support, progress and clear goals), **progress** was the number one performance motivator. To qualify as **meaningful,** the work has to matter to you.

What does making Meaningful Progress do?
- It triggers a **sense of accomplishment** and other positive perceptions, emotions and motivations.
- It increases **intrinsic motivation** (see below) when you make progress that serves a meaningful purpose.
- It leads to more **creativity,** higher **productivity** and more **commitment.**

How do you craft opportunities for Meaningful Progress in your days? Meaningful progress is enabled by:
- Setting clear **intentions** – so it connects perfectly with the previous tool.
- **Scheduling** time for work and rest.
- **Preparation** – collecting the resources you'll need, enabling you to get to it quickly or picking up where you left off.
- **Celebration** – marking the moment of achievement.
- Meaningful, clear **metrics** – more on this on page 62.
- **Support** or protection from *hindrance* and *interruption.*

> Meaningful progress is strongly related to **intrinsic motivation,** defined in Daniel Pink's research by three common elements:
> - **Purpose** – our innate need for connectedness and being part of something larger than ourselves.
> - **Autonomy** – our need for self-determination and the ability to direct our own lives.
> - **Mastery** – our desire to learn, grow and create in the work that we do.

Tool: Meaningful Progress

When reviewing the day with Design Notes, I want to focus on the most important craftwork accomplished to build a sense of flourishing and achievement. I also want to deepen my identity as a Day Crafter and my growing experience of autonomy, purpose and mastery.

What is it:

A sentence or a metric in Design Notes (but possibly more if you have time and motivation) that reviews *Meaningful Progress* made during the day. This could be general progress or a specific outcome related to a Day's Intention set for the day or Project (see page 84). It could even be related to your values or purpose – such as exercising generosity or helping a colleague.

Use it to:

Quickly instil a sense of accomplishment and other positive perceptions, emotions and motivations. These lead to an increase in intrinsic motivation, which is enhanced when you progress, particularly as it relates to the Design Objective Identity (page 75). This, in turn, leads to more creativity, higher productivity and more commitment.

As you set intentions for the day, how do you craft opportunities for Meaningful Progress?

Meaningful Progress can be enabled by,
- Clear intention
- Deep work time
- Preparation
- Celebration
- Metrics
- Support

Alternative measurement metrics for Meaningful Progress other than notes in Design Notes are crosses on a wall chart, moving objects from one container to another, turning a die to the following number. These more visual or tactile methods may be more motivating. Don't settle on one system. Try a variety.

The Progress Loop

Within Amabile's work on Meaningful Progress is the idea of progress loops. A Day Crafting interpretation of these would be that a crafted day with a healthy 'Quality of Inner Life' gives the next day a better foundation for achieving the same, so the progress loop strengthens.

The opposite is also the case. If a day is derailed and the quality of your inner life is poor, then the next day is vulnerable to the same.

Intention, Quality of Inner Life and Meaningful Progress reinforcing a positive loop across days.

 How are your days vulnerable to being derailed?

As we've explored previously, if you can orientate yourself from product to process, your days take on a different emphasis. Still, new challenges emerge, especially if we extend the progress loops to multiple, sequential days. If we focus on *systems of practice* and *process*, we may encounter some common problems.

- **Boredom.** Practising sometimes means doing the same thing repeatedly, and we need some way to cope with the monotony or reframe the issue.
- **Progress plateaus.** Development and improvement can appear slow or non-existent, and motivation to continue is hard to find. Progress always plateaus, so try measuring a different metric – see the next section.
- **Self discipline.** We may view ourselves as lacking this ingredient, which we imagine we will run out of.

This is true for anyone making long-term progress, so Day Crafting can only help. Identifying and overcoming these hurdles could be the skills you need to develop, the *problem* you're ready to *solve*.

Meaningful Progress from small, quick wins

Even small wins count as Meaningful Progress. They can come from quantifiable metrics or from interactions with others or even moments of inner pride; when you're pleased with yourself.

Reviewing your recent past – what qualifies as Meaningful Progress for you? Be expansive, look in less obvious places.

Our updated **Design Notes** example might look as simple as this. I write a capital MP in a box to note the Meaningful Progress. It is worth pointing out that Meaningful Progress can come from anything in your day, not necessarily the Day's Intention.

Tuesday 2 Nov 2021

2️⃣ After I load the dishwasher, I will read some of my new book

MP I read for 20 minutes with only one interruption – go me!

Creative ways to measure progress

Capturing Meaningful Progress in your Design Notes at the end of the day is practical and easy but there are some complementary practises that you may find more suitable in different circumstances and more motivating to you personally.

What you want to count is up to you. It could be time reading, standing up, miles run, healthy habits, mindful minutes, weight lost, or time devoted to focussed work. The value of this idea is to have a way to visualise the accumulation of gradual progress.

Try different methods periodically, as variety can help a strategy like this remain effective.

- **Dice.** A Day Crafting apprentice called Nick uses an eight-sided dice to count the glasses of water he drinks during the day.
- **Colouring In.** My daughter Gracie colours in one section of an illustration from a colouring-in book for every 15 minute guitar practise she completes.
- **Wall charts.** A lot of people like the visual aspect of a chart on the wall that you use to count (whatever it is you're making progress on) with big red Xs. Uninterrupted Xs make a 'streak'.
- **Marbles.** Move a marble from one jar to another to mark progress on a project.
- **Lego.** Build a tower or a model where each piece represents one unit that you're measuring.

You can also use this technique to count or monitor things you don't want to do, like destructive or annoying habits. I have found this particularly psychologically effective.

I wanted to cut out unintentional clicks to social media during challenging creative desk-based work. I used a six-sided dice to count and discovered that my elephant doesn't like being on notice this way – which was visually obvious with the dice number uppermost in front of me. This hack was immediately successful, and only a couple of times has the dice even reached 2 – I'm not sure what I would have done had it gotten to six.

Making progress visible

It's important to measure small, incremental progress; otherwise, it can be hard to see. Many outstanding achievements and inspiring changes are built one step at a time, and when you're focusing on the steps, you can miss the wow factor and motivational impact of the progress you're making – so maybe give this idea a go.

Adapting and making your own tools

Craftspeople have always needed to adapt or make tools for bespoke uses. My mother (a potter) had old bank cards cut to profiles to shape clay in particular ways. Carpenters adapt handles vices and clamps from materials to hand to better suit specific requirements the original tool makers could not envision ...

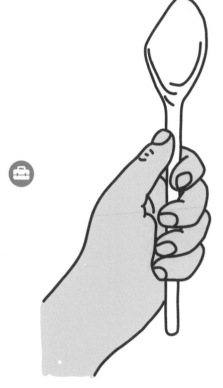

The kitchen, as a workshop, is another place for tool improvisation. We have a small collection of wooden spoons adapted for specific uses. I made this one (with saw + sandpaper) to make scrambled eggs in one particular pan – the flat edge scrapes the bottom of the pan in a way the curved edge couldn't.

The craftsperson identifies a problem that no tool to hand will solve – so they invent a new one.

I encourage you to adopt this thinking in your Day Crafting work. For example, many Day Crafting apprentices add their own intentions to the Day's Intention tool, and, as suggested on the previous page, progress can be measured in many creative and meaningful ways. My dice hack was hastily put together from a sticky note and a dice that happened to be on my desk.

In the craftsperson's workshop, all tools solve a specific problem. They work best when you're clear about *why* you're using a tool ... (unless you're playing). All Day Crafting tools descriptions roughly follow this *user story* format:

When (situation, problem, task), I want to (motivation, objective), so I can (expected outcome), and what else (more profound effect).

After two weeks practise

How long have you taken to reach this point? We would be at the two-week stage if you were taking the Day Crafting Apprentice Course. There is so much value to find in the basics we've covered so far, and you only really find that value through experience – your own practice will provide you with insight and wisdom.

Have you taken the time to do the basic workbook exercises and thought experiments and used the tools enough to learn?

A few interesting dynamics become apparent after practice and tool use. You can begin to see what problems tools solve. Put that another way, you will start to be more precise about *why* you want to use a particular tool – and you may begin to see what problems you don't yet have a tool to solve. For example, what about those days when our Quality of Inner Life is derailed? What tools can help there? Do you see your elephant and rider at work?

Another dynamic is that your default habits will push back. Novelty is a good motivator for a while, but novelty must be replaced by something else, some other discipline if your Day Crafting practice is going to progress. If your practice depends on whether you feel like it, you're in for a struggle. I don't run because I *feel* like it; I run because *I'm a runner* – this is identity-based practice.

Don't give up. We have our days to live; there isn't any choice. You're the Labourer or the Architect. Your days are either happening *to you* or *by you,* so you may as well choose to develop intention and skill. Maybe you can find, as many craftspeople do, that the practice is its reward.

Learning and practising are different. The workbook is good for learning, but practice will teach you the most. If you don't take the time to practise, you will learn very little.

If you've been practising with the **Day's Intention** tool (page 43) for enough time to find its value and possibly adapt the tool with one or two of your own intentions ... now will be a good time for a radical enhancement to the tool by adding *expectations*.

Expectation

Interoception, prediction and expectation – We explored our energy budget earlier in the workbook (page 24). We looked at the continual process of *interoception* that is happening in your mind as your energy budget is assessed against *predicted* use.

At the lowest level of consciousness, when we bring our attention to it, this process shows up as 'affect'; our *mood* on the pleasant/unpleasant and calm/agitated scales. You can change this by imagining pleasant or worrying things and noticing, for example, that your pulse speeds up or your tension increases.

The *prediction* part of this functionality isn't always right (and can be incorrectly negative) and you can increase calm and positivity by carefully setting or correcting **expectations.**

If you notice you're experiencing an agitated and unpleasant mood, there may be valid reasons – on the other hand, your elephant-based predictions may be wrong and it's time to bring the rider in.

Tool: Day's Expectation (additions to Intentions)

When I contemplate the day or activity ahead, I want to challenge any bias I am carrying to avoid nonconsciously affecting the day negatively and, better still, be delighted by positive outcomes.

What is it:

A numbered list of expectations that can be used for various situations and circumstances. I add this list to the **Intentions** I have written out at the front of my Design Notes.

Use it to:

Challenge the frame or story you have for the day ahead. Sometimes, our expectations for a situation or, more generally, for the day ahead can be unnecessarily negative. Our nonconscious brain can influence events to steer them to a negative conclusion (confirmation bias). This tool is one way to begin priming and crafting an alternative experience.

11. **What encouragement do I expect today?**
12. **What positive expectation should be at the forefront of my mind?**
13. **Today I will notice kindness.**
14. **I am making space in my day for grace.**
15. **What damaging expectations can I drop for today?**
16. **Can I drop any negative ideas that I am looking to confirm?**
17. **Today I will experience moments of peace and awe.**
18. **Today I am receptive to wisdom, insight or answers.**
19. **Today I trust ...**
20. **It's going to be a great day.**

I have my list of Day's Intentions and additional Expectations written on the inside cover of my Design Notes for easy access and reference. With space left for more to come ...

I don't choose a Day's Expectation as much as I choose a Day's Intention, but they are critical for certain circumstances.

Work in **progress** isn't supposed to be **perfect** ... or look good.

Relax into beginning; enjoy the **process** as it deepens.

Motivation to **practise** is more important than skill.

Look for the **problem**, don't over-focus on the solution.

Why is balance important?

Balanced days are the stable foundation and the prerequisite for a flourishing life which maximises energy, self-esteem, optimism, purpose and behaviour. Balance is the foundation for whatever you want Day Crafting for: greater productivity, more effective rest, increased wellbeing, or more stable life changes.

I'm not suggesting that balance is always easy to find or that everything will suddenly be perfect if it is achieved (perfection is unrealistic, but the rider doesn't always understand that). What *can* be achieved with balance, without too much skill, are small wins and Meaningful Progress – which are fantastic outcomes. I know that if I look after the balance of my days and the day that I'm living, the flourishing life will be much easier.

We can monitor balance during the day and remedy it if necessary. Managing balance skilfully is a good candidate focus for a Day Crafting apprentice whilst more specific problems are diagnosed.

 How do we balance our day, and how do we know when it is?

We need a simple diagnostic tool to help us tell if our day is out of balance and where to focus effort if it is.

The next section of the workbook will explore this.

The possibility and importance of balancing our days was one of the original motivations for creating Day Crafting. I was once part of a small team of facilitators, taking a group of leaders through a development process. We were intensely exploring their days, their lives, and their time management, and the topic of the necessity for holidays came up. One of the other facilitators mentioned that the monks following the Benedictine Rule didn't have or need holidays as all that was required for the 'balanced life' was within each day – enough work, enough rest and leisure, enough study and development, etc. Whilst this argument needs some unpacking (it is not suggesting that every day is a monotonous carbon copy of the previous day) there is a lot of wisdom in the idea, even at face value.

In craftwork only what gets measured gets improved – including balance

Metrics

We will get back to the specific question of measuring balance on the next page, but first, we will explore the broader need for craftspeople to be able to measure improvements to the quality and skill of their work – balance being just one example.

Is anything about your day already measured?

Perhaps more than you think. Mobile devices measure our activity and smart watches measure health metrics. Shops and digital banking count our spending and what we've purchased; our electricity and power use by our utilities; our journeys and location are measured through various GPS-enabled devices. Calendars and diaries record our tasks. Our web browsing and TV viewing history is measured, and even a bit of cardboard measures your reading progress in your book.

Many metrics benefit the companies you are a customer of, but this section is about taking control and finding metrics that help you and your development.

What defines a good Day Crafting measuring tool and metric?

1. It should only measure something you can do something about, called **actionable metrics.**
2. It has to measure only what matters. We need to know, '*What would I do with this information if I had it?*'. If confused, don't measure it.
3. It has to be simple and quick to use, or else you won't bother.

How do you measure or reflect on your day meaningfully and constructively? You're assessing yourself, after all.

Measuring, particularly qualitative and subjective aspects of your day, is far from straightforward; reviewing your day requires overcoming some issues. Read through the following four common self-assessment issues and assess to what degree you think they're issues for you on the 1 – 7 rating scale.

The first issue is that **we measure ourselves overly negatively.** Positive psychology research shows that when people rate the past day or a recent day, they rate it more negatively than if they measured events and circumstances in the present moment. To what degree do you have this negative bias?

Not an issue   O   O   O   O   O   O   O   A big issue

The second issue is that some of us **disqualify positives.** We think, for example, 'that nice thing only happened to me *by accident*', or we say to a friend, 'they only complemented me because *you* were standing here'.

Not an issue   O   O   O   O   O   O   O   A big issue

The third issue is that **negative events have an effect on us that is 5x stronger** than positive events. When reviewing the day it can be hard to balance negative and positive. Is this an issue for you?

Not an issue   O   O   O   O   O   O   O   A big issue

And the last issue is that we can **optimise for what we measure to create a vanity metric** to *fake* the results we want.

Not an issue   O   O   O   O   O   O   O   A big issue

Self-awareness is valuable but more tricky than we imagine, and your own opinion, your *internal* self-awareness, can benefit from an *external* perspective to counter your inbuilt inaccuracies.

In other words, **ask one or more people who know you well how they would assess you on the four issues above** and try to address any significant discrepancies between your and their assessments in your Day Crafting review work.

In your design review work, how can you mitigate any of the above issues you've scored high on as you assess and measure your progress?

Design Objectives

The model below sits at the heart of many Day Crafting tools. It represents all the elements that matter to our days condensed into four simple metrics. Our days are balanced across all four. It is simple enough that once you've learned what each section represents and further personalised each objective, you can use Design Objectives in a range of ways: Quickly as a mental dashboard to read your day right now, to review the day at the end – but also as an ultimate description of the identity of the person you are becoming. More on this shortly.

```
                Purpose



Quality of                    Quality of
Inner Life                    Actions and
                              Behaviour



              Maintenance
```

Maintenance

This first design objective is the foundation and support for all the rest. It is how you keep your body and mind going and your energy up, physical, mental, emotional and spiritual.

Quality of Inner Life (QIL)

In this objective, you have your thoughts and emotions, your self-talk and attention and focus – and crucially, where you interpret what happens, your mindset and framing. It is also where mindfulness and inner aspects of faith and hope reside.

Quality of Actions and Behaviour (QAB)

This is where work and doing, productivity and physical action are, where behaviours and habits are. It is your interaction with your environment and with those around you.

Purpose

This objective is about your focus but also your soul, heartfulness and generous living. It may be your calling, mission, or spirituality, but on a daily scale. What you're able to give to the world through service.

Each section is important and interdependent; we can't neglect any of them. Each interrelates, so the divisions are porous.

They're called *objectives* because this is ultimately how the tool is used; as a definition of what high quality looks like. In time, you will develop your explanation of what high-quality days mean for you in each of these and begin to work skilfully towards those *objectives*. It is designed to allow you to quickly draw it in your Design Notes using the Design Objective Review tool on page 68.

It has several uses. The most obvious is a quick diagnostic dashboard to assess a day's **balance** and see where remedial attention is needed. This often reveals a pattern where one section is out of balance consistently and needs more considered attention and experimentation design.

This model also forces a change of view, a different **perspective.** In craftwork production (in our case, crafting our days) the whole process is often too complex to see. It is easy to get drawn into detail, such as the practical task in front of you, or to get drawn into what's easy, enjoyable, or even problematic, so this forced pulling back can highlight areas you're not seeing.

The majority of our attention should be on the material at hand and the process of transformation, but you're also running the whole workshop, not just the project on the workbench – for example, your day and your life are not in balance if you're focussing on production in QAB but neglecting Maintenance.

This balanced overview and perspective are also essential as we **change.** Typically, change may fit into one of these four areas, but it doesn't happen in a vacuum. Change in one area can lead to unexpected changes in others – or change in one area may be deliberately about enabling change in another.

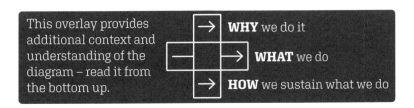

This overlay provides additional context and understanding of the diagram – read it from the bottom up.

→ **WHY** we do it

→ **WHAT** we do

→ **HOW** we sustain what we do

This page includes a number of questions to prompt you to think further about each of the four Design Objectives and how they relate specifically to you. Design Objectives will be a central component and metric for balancing and reviewing days.

 What happens when you're low in Maintenance?

What happens when you're low in QIL?

What happens when you're low in QAB?

What happens when you're low in Purpose?

If you need further inspiration around these four areas and which cause you problems – you've already given this some thought.

On page 16 you completed the Problem Hunting exercise. Questions 1 – 5 are about Maintenance, 6 – 10 are about the Quality of Inner Life; questions 11 – 15 are about the Quality of Actions and Behaviours and 16 – 20 are about Purpose.

Which is the most challenging for you to keep in balance?

Which is the most important one for you right now and why?

In which are you most vulnerable to losing balance and how?

Which would you like to work on more, or learn more about?

All craftspeople need to measure the quality of their work. From time to time, I want to more systematically and thoroughly review the balance of my days to highlight where progress is being made and expose neglected areas; a well-crafted day considers all four objectives. It also forces me to think more accurately about myself.

What is it:

A simple score for each Design Objective at the day's end during design review, to provide insight and actionable feedback.

Use it to:

Get a measure for a run of days, across a week or more. Once you've internalised and personalised the four objectives, you can also use it as a mental dashboard during the day to course-correct.

Use*: When reviewing a day, usually at the end of the day, score each Design Objective, from -2, -1, 1, 2 and put the total in the centre. For example:

See the table opposite as a starting point. Copy and paste the table into your own Design Notes. Better still, create your own version. Feel free to adapt and personalise this tool, which is easier to do if you've worked out what a good day looks like (the top score) in each of these four areas for you personally.

* Having tried a variety of metrics (for example, 1 - 10), I find the simplified 4-step range meaningful for me. I prefer to have a clear definition for each score, but I don't want to have to write 10 x 4 definitions. I use - and + to help me identify a line I hope to be above. 1s and 2s are good.

Another way of doing this is to define what 10 / 10 would be for each objective *(not a bad definition)* and then subjectively review your days from 1 to 10 based on that top-perfect score. Don't discount the possibility of designing a day that gives you a 10 in each – that has to be one ambition for Day Crafting!

	Maintenance	Quality of Inner Life	Quality of Actions & Behaviour	Purpose
2	**Excellent energy and resilience from good natural sleep, appropriate exercise and food – and from balanced and restorative activities during the day.**	**Strongest inner wellbeing, positive emotions and mental state sustaining focus and presence. Very best coping with turbulent situations.**	**Achieved intentions through skilled productivity, good habits and high quality actions. Savoured pleasure. Strong sensory connection with the working surface.**	**Acted with generosity, grace and heartfulness, exercised thankfulness and forgiveness. Living authentically with one's mission and calling.**
1	Energy okay or average. One maintenance detail neglected. Feeling a bit tired from time to time or that the tank isn't quite full.	Inner life was neutral. Perhaps a moment of mental or emotional turbulence or distraction but able to function nevertheless.	A normal day. Results of actions and behaviours were okay. Physical skills needing some effort to achieve their best.	Mild sense that opportunities for heartfulness were missed. Priorities partially compromised, purpose not central.
-1	Energy low enough to detrimentally affect other design details. Neglected some sleep, exercise and / or good nutrition and restorative activities. Likely negative effect on following days.	Negative mood, emotions, motivation or coping. Distracted by turbulent inner state. Unable to focus much. Thoughts captured by past or future. Rarely present.	Disappointed with what very little was actually achieved. Out of touch with senses and little pleasure felt. Seemingly, a partial loss of physical skill, not at one's best.	Lost sense of purpose and control. Noticeably selfish or egoic behaviour. Lashing out, being unkind. Avoiding opportunities for heartfulness.
-2	Lowest energy due to multiple causes. Unable to function or sustain other areas of life. Survival mode.	Very worst turbulent inner state, unable to focus. Thoughts totally captured and/or emotions hijacked. Not present.	Failure at practical work. Dominated by bad habits. Any action carried out resulted in worse outcome. No pleasure.	Living in opposition to one's authentic purpose and calling. Creating harm. Living destructively.

Minimalist Design Notes

We can now assemble several tools to form a simple and basic routine that takes no more than a few minutes of Design and Design Review time, typically at the beginning and end of the day (see page 39 for a reminder).

This simple Day Crafting routine now combines three tools:

- **Day's Intention (or Expectation)** from page 43
- **Meaningful Progress** from page 49
- **Design Objective Review** from page 68

We can revisit and update our Design Notes example. Here it is at the design stage; this is in the morning as I'm scheduling the day.

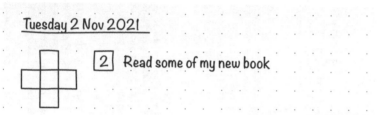

I start with the date and draw the outline for the Design Objective Review. This is always close to the outside edge of the page (so it's on the right on a right page) so that it is easy to scan pages to see how the metrics change over several days. The number in the box is the Day's Intention or Expectation (if you use the tool).

And at the end of the day, it looks like this in Design Review, complete with Meaningful Progress and Design Objective metrics.

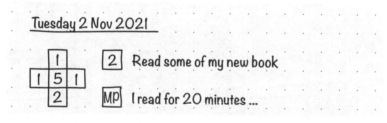

The page opposite gives you a six-day minimalist Design Notes template, which you can use, copy or replicate in your Design Notes. If you want to track five days or seven, that is up to you. I usually and deliberately take one day away from formal design thinking, the Self-care workbook explores that topic in more detail.

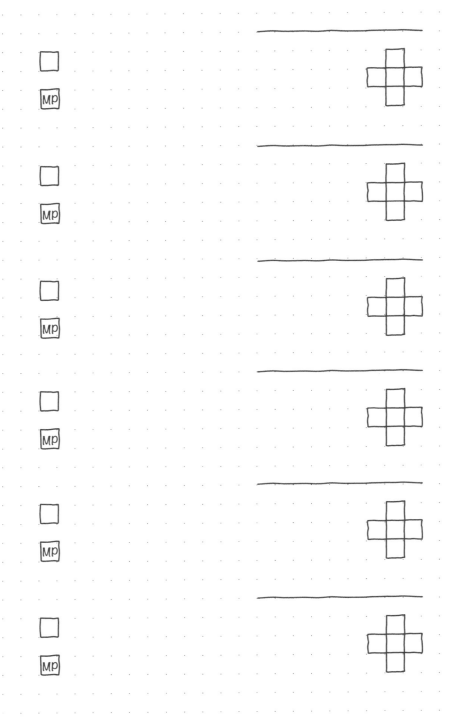

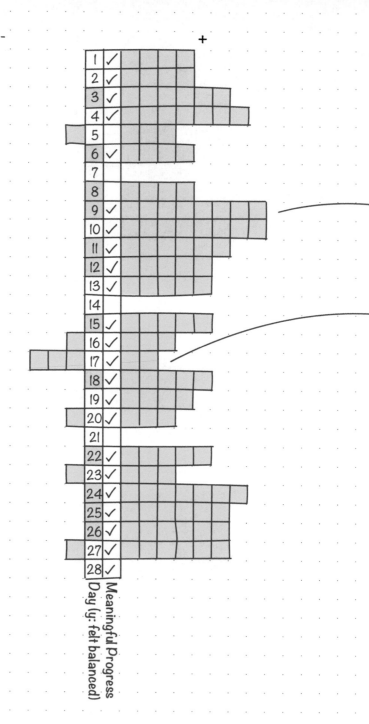

Purpose

QAB

QIL

The maximum possible totals over 24 days.

Maintenance

Most skilful day	Learning ...
	This was a wonderful day, everything went well. The main learning was to prepare in advance for the event and to make sure I was well rested beforehand.

Most skilful day grid:

	2	
2		2
	2	

Least skilful day	
	This day didn't go brilliantly. Main learning was around low QIL score and Purpose. An appraisal about poor customer feedback put me into a bad mood. I could have been better prepared ...

Least skilful day grid:

	-1	
-2		1
	1	

Celebrate whenever ...

			✓	✓	3 x QIL at 2 in a row
	✓	✓	✓	✓	Overall score ≤ 7
✓	✓	✓	✓	✓	Overall score better than previous day
			✓	✓	6 Meaningful Progress in a row
				✓	12 + days in balance

Once you've used the **Design Objective Review** tool for some time, you will have some data you can play around with in your **Design Notes.** Use your imagination. This page shows *my experiments* with metrics to illustrate what is possible. On the left is a graph with plus and minus scores taken from each day's review. That graph then provides inspiration for the overall totals for each Design Objective ... and further notes lower down. You can draw your data creatively to enable further learning.

Identity based development

We craft change in different ways at different levels. At the surface is outcome or goal-based change. Below that is practise and behaviour-based change. Deeper still is identity and belief. Put simply, the three are what you make, how you make it and your identity. The latter two go in tandem in Day Crafting but are not equal – *identity is the more powerful driver*.

Intentions and behaviours strengthen identity, but they're unlikely to embed if they do not align with who you think you are. If unsupported, they may last for a while, but our default ways will resume dominance.

But those default ways, our deeper identity, personality and beliefs, are not fixed; they are as mouldable as clay. If we can intentionally redefine our identity, our practice and behaviours towards the outcomes we want will be more straightforward, if not automatic.

> Stronger than our **intention** is our **identity**

A development of identity is not a surface dressing, nor is it something to acquire in the future. It is more like an uncovering or becoming by degrees. And it isn't a project that is ever finished; whatever vision we're inspired to become more like, we may realise, but there is always further to go. It is not difficult to start; replace a limiting belief you have about yourself with a positive one. Celebrate intentions met. Any Meaningful Progress strengthens the identity. Reinforce the intended identity through supportive feedback, knowledge and practice – who do you want to be today?

A word of caution about this work: beware of *opposition*, people possibly close to you who're invested in who you were, who may not like you changing because their security is based on a set version of you where you remain the same.

Another caution is that identity can work against us. Each time you repeat a statement such as: I'm really bad at … or not good at … or terrible at … you reinforce a negative identity.

The tool below is a simple way to explore identity using the four elements of the Design Objective.

Tool: Design Objective Identity
Change and growth through Day Crafting is about *identity* and *systems* of practice, not about future goals. Whenever related questions arise, such as – Am I being who I want to be? – I want to clearly understand what 'high quality' looks like to define problems and tools to work towards improvement.
What is it:
An ideal definition of yourself in each of the four Objective areas. This could be your description in the Design Objective Review tool on page 68. Write to capture your definitions in whatever way suits you. I recommend using present-tense first-person language.
Use it to:
Work out who you're becoming. It is how we are coming short of the Objective we have set ourselves that we find clarity about what to do in Day Crafting.

The ideas of the Labourer and the Architect are ways to explore identity. And of course, so is the idea of the craftsperson:

What is the identity of a craftsperson?

We design with knowledge, develop skill with **Play**, not knowing quite what the finished object is yet. With **Preparation** we improve. We **Filter** in order to focus on **Moments.** We aspire for a balance between quality and functionality. We feel pride in our work. We keep our tools sharp. We make tools that we need. We work with **Strengths** using minimum force. We're engaged and skilled. We're not in competition but in **Connection,** and we share insights. Our work benefits others. We may enlighten others more through showing than telling. Our work is original and bespoke. We make our days and we make ourselves.

Day Crafting is something that you do and something that you are.

Purpose, meaning and the sacred

Crafting identity to achieve growth, flourishing or change then links to mindsets and the triggering of desirable behaviours.

Previously, we looked at the Labourer and the Architect as identity archetypes. These are shortcuts to identity – for example, once we take on the identity characteristics of the Architect, our mindset shifts and our behaviour changes automatically – the identity permits us to act differently. Now, we can widen our thinking to include The Mystic among these archetypes. How is this mindset relevant to our Day Crafting?

There is room to explore the soul and the sacred in craftwork. For many craftspeople, there is a level of sacredness to what they do where the process and the product feel like they have a greater purpose. They've moved beyond the basics, focusing on tool-use and systems of practice, towards a deeper aspect of discovering and revealing meaning. This is different from making meaning as the Architect would view it. It is instead about discerning something that is at first indistinct and being a part of forming its shape, co-creating it.

This may seem philosophical and possibly theological for some – but it shouldn't make it rare and refined. It is a dynamic in the unstructured play of children (the precursor to elements of craft process); it is there in the feelings of flow and creativity that is the experience of many craftspeople, from carpenters to coders.

We accept and forgive ourselves for being like the Labourer and instead put our efforts into being like the Architect – but there is a whole new level to explore through the Mystic.

The Mystic

'Today is happening **through me.**'

- Central to the *to me* or *by me* mindset is *me*. Something *other* or *more significant* is central to the *through me* mindset.

- Control and responsibility only carry us so far – there is a lot more beyond.

- Curiosity, creativity, transcendence, awe, surprise and peace open up.

- Often, worry and stress begin to diminish. Acceptance of *what is* can be powerful and liberating.

- The craftsperson begins to discern the ability to reveal that the meaning in life, at the working surface, is situated outside of themselves.

Do you find this mindset appealing, challenging, scary or even nonsensical?

What practises enable you to support this mindset?

Control or Surrender

Autonomy is crucial for Meaningful Progress, deep work, and deep play. Autonomy, being able to choose and have control, adds to our wellbeing. External authorities permit this control – for example, your boss may give you more responsibility and control at work. Autonomy is also a subjective and internal point of view; it is part of identity and mindset.

The *Labourer* has little or no control, as a fact of his job and a self-limiting view of himself. The *Architect* is having none of *that!* She's pushing to gain more autonomy and control by widening her sphere of influence and developing her self-identity. For her, the shift is creative and exhilarating.

And now, here comes the *Mystic* who says that to go further, we need to surrender – just when we were enjoying the empowerment of being the Architect. The Mystic hears a call to travel beyond independence through trust to *interdependence*.

Remember that Day Crafting is as small as one simple thing you can do now or with the rest of today – or a simple one-day experiment. That is an excellent way to explore this facet of craftwork; see if this idea inspires or resonates with you.

If you find the Architect more relevant to how you are in your life currently, then come back to this later.

People who craft their days with a *through me* mindset often do so within a supportive community. The conscious intention to live this way is strengthened through support and schedules designed to cope with the particular challenges this intention brings. It is possible to do this in isolation, and it is great to bring this into daily crafting, but the fullest expression is challenging without community or a supporting culture.

Tool: Day's Surrender (additions to Intentions)

When my perception of the day's challenges or opportunities meet a particular threshold, or my senses suggest it, I want to frame the day with a *'through me'* mindset to remind myself that what I can control isn't the ultimate expression of skilful craftwork.

What is it:

A numbered list of Surrender intentions that can be used for various situations and circumstances. I add this list to the Intentions and Expectations I use in my Design Notes.

Use it to:

Give your day to something bigger than yourself.

The Architect has a healthier mindset than the Labourer. Purpose for the Architect is defined by 'What do I want?'. She stops, works it out, and makes it happen. For the Mystic, he thinks: 'What purpose or idea does life* have to create in and through me?'. The Mystic doesn't try to work it out, he listens and waits.

21. **Make me a channel for peace.**
22. **Today I trust, body, mind and soul.**
23. **Today, your will, not mine be done.**
24. **In my own strength I can do nothing.**
25. **Today I realise that I am not alone.**
26. **Today I accept what is.**
27. **Today I yield all things.**
28. **By letting it go it all gets done.**
29. **I have all that I need.**
30. **Whatever happens, happens on time.**

Life could be substituted with *love*, *God*, *presence* or *universe*.

Surrender starts with letting go of *wanting* to be in control [just for today]. **Explore how you think and feel about this idea from three perspectives:**

What are the **pluses** about the idea?

What are the **minuses** about the idea?

What is **interesting** about the idea?

This **PMI** *critical thinking* tool was devised by Edward de Bono

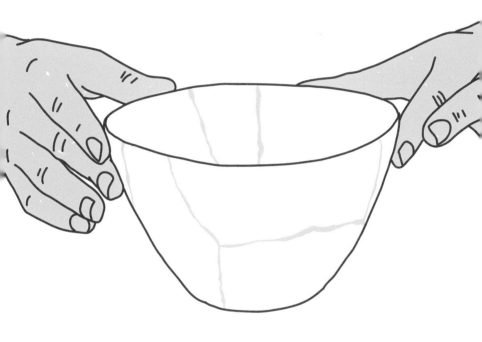

Japanese craft of kintsukuroi
or golden repair – where being broken is only
a step towards greater things.

Design Notes Journalling

The *minimalist* Design Notes design and review tools, mentioned on page 70, could take as little as a minute or two per day, but there is treasure to be found by spending *more* time in design thinking, particularly in review, typically later in the day or during the weekend when our thinking is more focused, relaxed and creative and we feel more time affluent.

There are lots of approaches and techniques for periodic journalling ranging from – *just write a page* to design thinking tools like *mind-mapping.* I find the benefits come if I'm clear about *why* I'm choosing to journal. If I'm not clear, if I don't have a problem to solve or insight to find, then I don't pick the tool up. Some common benefits of periodic journalling include ...

- **Reflective practice.** Adults learn through experience, design and craft, but only through reflection on the learning loop: *design, craft, review ...*
- **Capturing better stories to tell.** The moments worth remembering can be captured on or close to the day they happened to aid recall.
- **Insight.** Knotty problems or nagging issues, competing priorities or difficult decisions – journalling helps untangle and clarify thinking.
- **Perspective.** Some exercises, see the Insight tool opposite, force a change in perspective, which develops wisdom and widens and informs future choices.
- **Discovering meaning.** What is meaningful and essential to you is vital to your Day Crafting, steering your intentions and Purpose.
- **Redefining identity.** New understanding of self-image, personality and emotion shows that these are adaptable and can be changed – and reflection helps that process.
- **To unburden.** Write to bear witness, remember, heal, externalise, and share what might be weighing heavy on your mind.

Spend time in your journal and your journal will teach you everything!

When I feel the need, I want to explore my thoughts, so I can stretch and find insight and answers, and find the depths of QIL only this work can bring.

What is it:

Journalling (writing or design thinking) in search of an answer, often found tangentially through a prompt (see below) or lateral thinking excursion**.

Use it to:

Use one of the following questions, or your own, to prompt writing or mind-mapping for reflection.

1. **What have I learned today?**
2. **What was enough for today, what was lacking?**
3. **I will write the words I need to hear.**
4. **What were the small wins today?**
5. **How would a wise and compassionate observer review my day? ***
6. **How would my 8 or 25 year old self review my day? ***
7. **How will I think about this day in a month? ***
8. **Where was I most skilful, what energized me?**
9. **What feelings or thoughts can I let go of?**
10. **If I lived today again, what would I do differently?**
11. **Describe a new Design Objective Identity. See page 75.**
12. **Formulate a Project for the coming days. See page 84.**
13. **Was there a significant pivot point?**
14. **What can I write so that I go to bed contented?**

* Insight questions 5, 6 & 7 all use a change of perspective. This can be temporal (how today will seem in a month), a shift in identity (wise friend) – or both (younger you). The identity change can be particularly useful if you're trying to solve a creative problem. How might a detective, primary school teacher, monastic, gangster, scientist, film director, etc. see this problem?

** Excursions: creative prompts to dislodge our thinking.

Here are four more valuable tools. The first one, Projects, is used during the design stage (thinking ahead) and the other three are for design review (thinking back to the day past). Use these tools to help develop your ongoing Day Crafting practice.

Projects

There is nothing quite so lovely for the craftsperson as getting into a groove of process and practice for a run of time, perhaps for two weeks.

A Project is not too long, so progress gets lost or goes off track, nor so short that progress doesn't seem to happen at all. There is a rhythm to Projects that balances getting on with it with a healthy cadence of stopping to review direction.

An example Project: Overcome distraction. Exercise daily. Memorise a suit / deck of cards. Read a book. Keep a gratitude diary. Schedule every day / hour / ½ hour / minute. Drop off social media. Detox from something. Get good sleep.

Tool: Projects

When thinking about intentions, I often want to focus on the same intention for some time to make more Meaningful Progress and simplify or eliminate the morning Design Notes, Day's Intention setting routine.

What is it:

A Project is the same intention used every day for a run of days, usually two weeks.

Use it to:

In your Design Notes, write one intention and some details about it for the Project. I write a capital **P** in the box I would otherwise write the Day's Intention number in for the duration of the Project – usually two weeks, but it can vary.

This is an excellent tool to link Intention with Meaningful Progress. It also removes the challenge of asking yourself each morning what the Intention for the day should be. Two weeks is a good length to see accumulated Meaningful Progress – and possibly an opportunity for celebration or reward.

Unskilful / Skilful

The craftsperson aspires to work skilfully, evidenced in the process of making the finished product. When reviewing the day, this idea of skill use provides you with a different frame than we've used so far to learn from the day.

How skilful were you in your Day Crafting? How skilful were you as you reacted to something unexpected? Where are you pleased with your skill use today? Where were you unskilful? Where do you need to work on developing skills?

Tool: Unskilful / Skilful

When reviewing a complex day, I want to categorise my craftwork so I can quickly see what issues need thought and attention, find where the learning is and make complicated problems more practical or actionable.

What is it:

Short bullet points or notes under each heading listing issues and accomplishments. They can be thoughts, actions, reactions, decisions, omissions etc.

Use it to:

As a craftsperson, use it to review skill and quality. This is not a moral list of good and bad or like and dislike but a more objective assessment.

Unskilful doesn't mean a failure, or wrong or bad. If anything, it is a gentle prompt for learning and development. Nevertheless, I usually note the unskilful aspects of my practice, ending on the more positive, skilful aspects, which we need to be more diligent about measuring.

Preparation and **Tools**

The last two tools for the Design Notes review work.

Tool: Preparation

When thinking about what comes next, I want to make future tasks easier to overcome inertia, prepare to react to challenges and distractions and be kind to *future* me.

What is it:

It can be anything that makes future tasks and behaviours easier. (The craftsperson keeps the workshop tidy, orders materials, and keeps their tools sharp.)

Use it to:

For example, if running in the morning is a challenge, put the running clothes out ready or even sleep in them. Preparation is part of the design and review loop when you know that tasks in the future will be made easier or only possible through preparation. Preparation is a pervasive idea in Day Crafting, so it is also one of the core *methods* explored in further workbooks.

Tool: Tools

When considering my effectiveness as a craftsperson, I want to make sure I'm acting skilfully and efficiently so I can work with effectiveness and economy of effort and enjoy the creativity of adapting tools or developing new ones.

What is it:

A note about some or all of the Day Crafting tools you used that day.

Use it to:

Review what is working and what isn't. Keep a list to see what you've tried and the outcomes. Clarify the need for your own tools.

A comprehensive Design Notes Layout

Compared to the previous minimalist layout, here is an example of a more thorough structure, including the tools introduced in the last few pages. This is an example rather than a template – you can develop your own more creative layout.

□
MP

- Unskilful	+ Skilful

Insight:

Preparation:

Tools:

Next Steps and *Deliberate* Practise

Practise Cadence

The skills that develop from the practice and experience of Day Crafting become more automatic and internalised over time. Experienced Day Crafters don't use *all* the tools all the time and don't necessarily use any tools *every* day. That is how a maturing practice is – but there is a danger that our default ways regain control after we've spent some time and passion learning the basics. We do no further deliberate or intentional work (the reasons for this were explored in the material section).

How do we balance mature, internalised Day Crafting and the need to revisit the basic disciplines to continue developing? What triggers us to return to conscious, deliberate development when we don't feel like it or progress has plateaued?

Continued improvements depends on **deliberate practice**

I love the periods of automatic, internalised and flowing Day Crafting, but I also maintain a discipline of a periodic, conscious revisiting of the basics (such as Day's Intention setting and Insight in my design notes), which are triggered in two ways.

Diary triggers: Every ... I will ...

Every week, month, or season (the regularity is up to you) you can make time to practise a particular aspect of Day Crafting (which is also up to you). *E.g. Every month, I will use the Design Objective Review tool for a week (if I've not used it for a while) to check how balanced my days are* – like an MOT.

Event or situation triggers: When ... I will ...

I have also prepared that if life brings along particular challenges, problems or situations, I will pause and become more deliberate with my practice. *E.g. When I am more tired than usual, I will revisit my maintenance disciplines.*

Have a go opposite, drafting your own practice cadence.

Some people find this kind of self-discipline difficult, but other ways exist to encourage ongoing deliberate practice by joining in with the growing community of other Day Crafters. See the 'next steps' described later in this section.

Practise Triggers

Every   I will ...

Every   I will ...

Every   I will ...

When   I will ...

When   I will ...

When   I will ...

Deliberate, Intentional, Purposeful Practice

A crucial skill is beneath the surface as you develop as a craftsperson as efficiently as possible and to your fullest potential. It isn't innate gifting or natural talent but is ongoing practice carried out in a particular way.

The wrong way to practise is to repeat something over and over and, even worse, do so without knowing why you're doing it.

The right way to practise is to be much more analytical about what specifically needs to be worked on and do this at the manageable edge of your comfort zone, motivated by why you want to make improvements in the first place.

This practice keeps us making Meaningful Progress and reinforces our commitment and enthusiasm to continue.

All the fundamental tools are in this workbook: intention setting, reviewing the results, clear metrics and progress that matters. The basic tools themselves are a way to make the practice effective, and the whole workbook has been about this kind of learning and development – from problem-hunting to design review tools.

Know your motivation

Ultimately it helps if you're clear about the **big, sparkly reasons why** you should continue your Day Crafting practice. There is space opposite for you to capture your reasons why.

Here are some optional questions to prompt your thinking.

- What does Day Crafting enable you to do differently?
- What is better about your days if you Day Craft them?
- What is different about you when you're Day Crafting?
- What changes would you like to craft in your days?
- What Day Crafting skills would you like to master?
- What would becoming a skilled Day Crafter achieve for you?
- What differences might other people notice about you?
- What are some unfulfilled Day Crafting goals?
- What would happen if you don't continue to practise?
- What days and outcomes do you want to avoid?

Why become a Day Crafter?

How much effort we give something depends on how important we think it is – the **why.** This is in your hands as a craftsperson. If you design, strengthen and prepare the **why** of your practice, the rest will be far easier.

Next steps

Hopefully this workbook has enabled you to begin your own rhythm of practise; design, craft and review. The workbook will have introduced you to enough tools to find value in that learning cycle. You're setting intentions, exploring where Meaningful Progress is being made, assessing your balance and progress and noticing how your mindset impacts all of this.

You can take your Day Crafting skills a long way with tools such as *Insight* and *Design Objective Identity* – and many apprentices find the *Day's Intention* tool consistently valuable.

But there is much more to explore and from here onwards you can tailor where you want to go next, what *you're* ready to learn.

MAPS
This monthly virtual gathering is for anyone who's completed the Apprentice Course or the Introductory Workbook. It is an opportunity to share ongoing learning with a like-minded community. If you'd like to join, use the contact form at daycrafting.com#contact

Online community
There is a private facebook group you can join if you would like to interact with a social community of fellow apprentices. It is also *a good place to ask questions* about any of the content in the workbooks facebook.com/groups/daycrafting

Workshop
A range of Day Crafting workshops are available by arrangement. As with any craft, workshop participants should be able to pick up useful skills and life-changing insights in even the shortest time. Workshops also include accessible content covering related theories and psychology. More information at daycrafting.com

1:1 Sessions
For the most in-depth support and progress, you can explore 1:1 support or guidance. More information at daycrafting.com

Further workbooks

This introductory workbook is self contained and gets an apprentice Day Crafter started. It includes some of the most valuable concepts and tools in the whole practice. However, in order to deepen your practise there are further workbooks to choose from.

Each of these builds on the introductory workbook and explores further specialisation. These will be available from the Day Crafting website where you can sign-up for an occasional newsletter to keep you informed of the latest insights in Day Crafting.

Day Crafting: The Body-clock Workbook
Designing days and harnessing the
power of your chronobiology
- The extraordinary benefits of scheduling
- The when-to-do list and the power of your circadian profile
- Designing blueprints and memorable moments

Day Crafting: The Productivity Workbook
Crafting practice for deep work and productivity
- Implementing process systems to produce results
- Applying craftwork rhythms to modern work-life
- Enabling productivity with rest and play

Day Crafting: The Self-care Workbook
Active rest and wellbeing for everyday flourishing
- Complementing deep work with deep rest
- Reviewing energy use to increase wellbeing
- Understanding our deeper need for connection

Day Crafting: The Change Workbook
Daily practise for growth, identity and behaviour change
- Multiplying the power of intention with attention
- Applying design thinking to habit formation
- Daily progress on character and personality shaping

Glossary and Subject Index
A glossary of terminology and an index of subjects and where they're covered in depth and in which workbook can be found at daycrafting.com/workbooks

PS: If you've found this workbook valuable, please leave a positive review on Amazon and Facebook and tell your friends. Thanks, BS.

Day Crafting is a framework for personal development that emphasises ...

- *working with chronorhythms, intention and attention*
- *skilled and meaningful use of time and energy*
- *raising typical performance*
- *crafting daily Meaningful Progress*
- *gentle rhythms of craftwork and mastery*
- *the good life is a practice, not a future destination*

You can use it to solve a problem or make it a part of your identity. You may then say, I don't do Day Crafting; *I am a Day Crafter.*

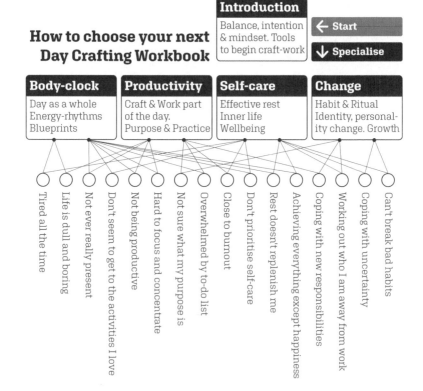

How to choose your next Day Crafting Workbook

Introduction
Balance, intention & mindset. Tools to begin craft-work

← **Start**

↓ **Specialise**

Body-clock
Day as a whole
Energy-rhythms
Blueprints

Productivity
Craft & Work part of the day.
Purpose & Practice

Self-care
Effective rest
Inner life
Wellbeing

Change
Habit & Ritual
Identity, personality change. Growth

- Tired all the time
- Life is dull and boring
- Not ever really present
- Don't seem to get to the activities I love
- Not being productive
- Hard to focus and concentrate
- Not sure what my purpose is
- Overwhelmed by to-do list
- Close to burnout
- Don't prioritise self-care
- Rest doesn't replenish me
- Achieving everything except happiness
- Coping with new responsibilities
- Working out who I am away from work
- Coping with uncertainty
- Can't break bad habits

Tools

Have used
Have used regularly
Have adapted

Made in the USA
Columbia, SC
03 June 2024

36257356R00057